Bringing it home

Government plans for an entitlement to early language learning pose an exciting challenge for all primary schools. CILT can help you to deliver that entitlement in school and support early language learning at home.

NACELL (the National Advisory Centre on Early Language Learning), established at CILT and on-line, offers you support through information on:

- what's happening in schools
- teaching resources
- training courses
- joining the ell-forum
- ELL Regional Support Groups
- publications, including the CILT *ELL Bulletin*
- the *European Language Portfolio*
- the *NACELL guide to best practice*

Bringing it home

How parents can support children's language learning

Anne Farren and Richard Smith

The views expressed in this publication are the authors' and do not necessarily represent those of CILT.

Acknowledgements

The authors and publisher would like to acknowledge the following for permission to reproduce copyright material: p22: 'Les escargots' and 'Il pleut' from *Jeux de doigts* (La Jolie Ronde Ltd, 2001). p26: 'Das ABC-Lied', by Lore Kleikamp and Detlev Jöcker from *Start German with a song* (Menschenkinder Verlag, Münster). p40: *A dark, dark tale* by Ruth Brown (Andersen Press), *'Une histoire sombre ... très sombre'* (French translation, Gallimard Jeunesse). p45: 'Learn 1 to 10' from www.quia.com. p46: 'J'ai vu un dinosaure' by Marie-Hélène Lafond, p48: 'Anniversaires', p50: 'Brochettte de fruits' and p61: 'Douce nuit, sainte nuit' from www.momes.net. p47: 'La galette des rois' from www.poulesfrites.com. p51: www.marie-saintromainlepuy.fr. p53: Cœur de Lion (La Compagnie des fromages). p55: Cheetos (Matutano). p56: Texas Hollywood; Hotel de la Loge, Perpignan. p62: 'Noël est proche' from www.jecris.com.

In some cases it has not been possible to trace copyright holders of material reproduced in this book. The publisher will be pleased to make the appropriate arrangement with any copyright holder whom it has not been possible to contact at the earliest opportunity.

First published 2003 by the Centre for Information on Language Teaching and Research (CILT)
20 Bedfordbury, London WC2N 4LB
Copyright © Centre for Information on Language Teaching and Research 2003
Illustrations by Kate Taylor. Part 1 photo © 2000, Barbara Ludman/iwitness
Cover design: Richard Vockins
ISBN 1 904243 19 3

A catalogue record for this book is available from the British Library

Printed in Great Britain by Hobbs the Printers Ltd, Totton, Hampshire

CILT Publications are available from: **Central Books,** 99 Wallis Rd, London E9 5LN. Tel: 0845 458 9910. Fax: 0845 458 9912. Book trade representation (UK and Ireland): **Broadcast Book Services,** Charter House, 27a London Rd, Croydon CR0 2RE. Tel: 020 8681 8949. Fax: 020 8688 0615.

contents

Introduction

As teachers of primary-age children, we have found out that learning is most successful when school and home are working together. By and large, parents are supportive of the broad aims of their children's schools but often need more information and guidance to help them support their children in appropriate activities when not in school. This is particularly true in the teaching of a foreign language where the methods and approaches used in the primary school may be very different from those that parents themselves experienced.

In its current form, the early teaching of a modern language is a comparatively new addition to the primary curriculum and one which is likely to have only a small amount of time allotted to it. Parents with some knowledge of the language being taught are ideally placed to provide the extra ongoing input that is not always possible in the busy primary timetable. They can contribute much, not only to the acquisition and use of language skills, but also to the sense of fun and motivation that can be a feature of learning and speaking a new language. Even with little or no knowledge of the target language, a great deal can still be offered using the simple activities described in this book. Indeed, the pleasure and motivation of a parent learning alongside their child can provide a real stimulus and an enjoyable context for both.

Families where another language is already spoken will approach the language being learnt at school as a **third** language. The existing richness of language knowledge in this situation provides opportunities to make links between English, the modern foreign language and the home language. For example, common features of early language use such as counting and nursery rhymes can be discussed and enjoyed. Whether or not another language is spoken at home, most children love to take their language learning home with them. They enjoy the opportunity to show off their new skills to others and will get extra motivation if this meets with responses which value what they have learnt and take it a little further.

In the school context a wide range of motivational activities including games, songs, tapes and videos, the Internet, drama and story-telling are used, and if children are to enjoy and be successful in their language learning, similar approaches should be used at home. We hope that the kind of activities and resources which are suggested in this book will be fun not only for the children but also for their parents.

Parents of children who go to schools where a language is **not** taught may be just as keen that they should gain some experience of language learning prior to secondary school. There is no reason why they should not use the sort of activities described in this book, provided that care is taken to ensure that their natural enthusiasm is encouraged and that they develop a positive attitude to language learning. In fact, whatever the situation, it is most important to ensure that any work done at home or on holiday does not become a chore. Activities that are enjoyed by everybody taking part will improve the child's knowledge of a different language and culture and show that the process of learning to speak the language can be pleasurable in its own right.

This book contains many ideas for activities suitable for parents to use at home or out and about to initiate, consolidate or develop their children's learning of a foreign language. We hope that it will also be of use to teachers both in schools where Foreign Language teaching is already taking place and in those where it is not. Many of the suggested activities can be used in the classroom by linguists and non-specialists alike. They might also provide ideas for teachers who wish to enlist the support of parents both at home and perhaps within school where the opportunity for children to work in a small group with an enthusiastic adult would be beneficial.

Languages in the primary curriculum

Languages do not form a part of the National Curriculum in England and Northern Ireland and it is not statutory to teach them. Nevertheless, the status of Modern Language teaching in primary schools continues to grow. The Government's proposal that every primary pupil in England should be entitled to learn a foreign language by 2010 offers a challenge to many primary schools in developing what to them may be a new area of the curriculum. Beginning to develop policies and practice now, even in a small way, will undoubtedly enable schools to meet future requirements more readily and confidently, and we hope that this book, with its emphasis on enjoyment and enthusiasm, will contribute towards this important development.

How to use this book

In Part One of this book, we consider the context of early language learning in Great Britain and describe the background to language teaching in primary schools. This includes a look at current guidelines and a consideration of what is being taught and how. Part Two describes practical activities that parents or teachers might like to undertake and presents ideas both of ways of learning and topics around which learning might be based. At the end of each chapter there is a 'Resources' section which includes websites, books, useful addresses, etc.

The activities described in this book can be used whatever language is being learnt. The majority of examples given are in French, reflecting the reality of foreign language teaching in primary schools at this time. We have given as many sources of further materials in other languages as we can.

Each chapter includes a quotation from a parent who has tried some of the suggested activities, affording a more personal viewpoint.

Finally, the order of the book is not intended to present a language-learning sequence. A good approach is to dip into the different chapters for activities that appeal and which seem appropriate to the child's level of ability and interests.

Parents often ask teachers 'How can I support my child's learning?'. We hope that this book will provide a resource from which parents can pick activities that are fun and motivating, and will complement work done at school. Although there may be no direct links between these activities and the foreign language curriculum of the school, it is intended that the nature and spirit of the content will help to enthuse both parents and children, and create a positive attitute towards language learning.

Our experience of working with primary children has shown us that there is a great deal of support and interest among parents, and that they are willing to try activities of the kind described here which may be very different from the homework tasks that they themselves experienced.

While activities suggested in this book have been selected as appropriate to use at home, often on a one-to-one basis, many of them could, of course, be adapted for use in the classroom.

what parents say ...

My daughter loves learning French at school and would really enjoy doing more activities of this kind at home. I think it's wonderful for children to have these opportunities.

(Parent of Simrin, 8)

part one

Language teaching in primary schools today

one

Who is learning a language in primary school?

In 2000 an independent inquiry into our national capability in languages within the United Kingdom was published by the Nuffield Foundation. The report argues that reliance on the English language is leaving young people from the UK at an increasing disadvantage in the international recruitment market. Among its recommendations it proposes that more children of primary school age should be given the opportunity to learn a foreign language. This earlier exposure to language learning will promote cultural diversity and understanding, and equip young people with the skills needed for the learning of additional languages later in life.

The extent and scope of teaching Foreign languages in UK primary schools varies both across and within the regions, reflecting national and local priorities.

A research report commissioned by the Qualifications and Curriculum Authority (QCA) in December 2000 indicates that approximately 21% of schools in England with Key Stage 2 pupils (ages 7–11) are providing access to a Foreign Language. This may be through timetabled lessons, extra lessons or clubs.

In England over the last ten years or so, despite the fact that there has been no nationally led initiative, the teaching of foreign languages in primary schools has gradually developed, often through the enthusiasm of individual headteachers, teachers, governors and parents. In some areas there have been successful local schemes, such as in Croydon, Kent or Richmond upon Thames. These have received varying levels of support and funding from their Local Education Authority. More recently, primary schools linked to specialist Language Colleges have benefited from shared resources, including specialist language teachers. Elliott School in Putney, Impington College in Cambridgeshire and Sir Bernard Lovell School in South Gloucestershire are among schools that have led the way in this respect.

It is against this background that the Department for Education and Skills (DfES) charged the Centre for Information on Language Teaching and Research (CILT) with co-ordinating an Early Language Learning Initiative in England and Wales, the first two-year phase of which was delivered from 1999 to 2001. This initiative, now in its second phase, seeks to provide advice and support to those schools interested in or already involved in teaching a foreign language, and to establish a basis for future developments. The National Advisory Centre for Early Language Learning (NACELL) was consequently set up as a dedicated area of CILT and is a useful source of information and advice – both resource centre and website (see 'Further sources of information' for contact details).

To bring Modern Languages into line with other subject areas of the Key Stage 2 curriculum, QCA published a non-statutory scheme of work for Modern Languages at Key Stage 2, in 2000. Many primary schools have found this to be a useful framework from which to develop their own teaching programmes. Some local education authorities such as Richmond upon Thames and West Sussex have also adapted the scheme for use in their schools, to ensure some level of consistency. The QCA scheme proposes ideas for twelve units of work that might be covered during the key stage although it is stressed that each school should adapt the material to suit its own context, such as the amount of time allocated to Foreign Languages. The complete set of units is offered in French, with some illustrated in German and Spanish. Whereas it is not our intention to suggest that you would find it appropriate to use the QCA scheme of work, you might find it of interest to have a look, in order to get an idea of the topics and activities that schools are typically using. This material can be viewed on the QCA website (**www.qca.org.uk**) and the list of topics covered is given on p13 of this book.

In March 2001, a QCA study examined the feasibility of introducing a foreign language into the statutory curriculum at Key Stage 2. This revealed four major issues impeding expansion on a national scale at this time, namely:

- the amount of time available in the primary curriculum;
- the availability of specialist foreign language teachers;
- the lack of places available to train primary teachers to teach a foreign language;
- progression in the foreign language between primary and secondary school.

Government proposals, announced in December 2002, seek to address these issues through a commitment to promote greater linguistic capability in England. The paper *Languages for all: languages for life* outlines proposals for phasing in an entitlement for all children aged 7–11 to learn at least one foreign language by 2010. Equally, it is proposed that children reach a nationally recognised level of competence at age 11. This will be part of a new scheme, as yet to be developed, to recognise the achievements of language learners at all ages.

The Welsh Assembly Government's national Foreign Languages strategy was published in April 2002. Within a context where all children are required to learn a second language from an early age, the study of English and Welsh is mandatory in all state primary schools. The Assembly Government will fund pilot schemes of foreign language learning at Key Stage 2, beginning in 2003. Funding will also be made available to develop guidance on how best to develop early language-learning experience as children move through to secondary school.

In Northern Ireland, there is currently no national policy, but if parents would like to investigate, they should contact their local Education and Library Board.

In Scotland the picture differs from elsewhere in the UK. The first phase of a national pilot scheme for Foreign Languages in Scottish primary schools was launched in 1989. Further national pilots and local authority initiatives to promote the teaching of French, German, Spanish and Italian followed. The Secretary of State for Scotland announced in 1992 that a foreign language would be introduced in every primary school over a five-year period. Over 90% of Scottish primary schools are now teaching a modern foreign language, with French as the dominant language. Some local authorities are experimenting with starting a foreign language in the earlier stages of primary school and with partial immersion (where some of the curriculum is taught through the medium of the foreign language).

what parents say ...

I wish Helen had learnt a language earlier because I think she would have picked it up really quickly. I didn't know that some junior schools were teaching it now or I might have pushed for it!

(Parent of Ellen, 11)

two

Why learn a foreign language in primary school?

The opportunity to learn a foreign language in primary school provides children with a rich educational experience as well as valuable social and cultural development. Learning how to communicate in another language extends a child's literacy skills and this means that, in addition to learning more about their own language, foundations for that child's future language learning are laid. Learning another language also opens up an international dimension to children, giving them insight into their own and other cultures.

Many of the recommendations and requirements laid down in the secondary national curricula for learning Modern Languages in the UK can be applied to primary school children. They can be introduced to techniques and strategies for how to understand and use the foreign language that will be developed further as they progress to secondary school, such as:

- listening carefully to discriminate sounds and identify meaning;
- developing accurate pronunciation and intonation;
- asking and answering questions;
- memorising words, phrases and short texts such as rhymes, poems and songs;
- using context and visual or non-visual clues to interpret meaning;
- making use of their knowledge of English or other languages that they know to help them learn.

As children develop further their knowledge, skills and understanding in the foreign language, they can also be given opportunities to consolidate this learning through:

- making the link between sounds and writing, for instance by listening to a story tape and following it in the book;
- applying some simple aspects of grammar, such as plurals;

- developing enough confidence to initiate conversations and using language for a real purpose, for example inviting another child to play or getting what they want in a café;
- finding new words or meanings using simple reference materials such as picture dictionaries in printed form or on CD-ROM.

It is important to realise that all of these techniques and strategies are also those that are vital to competence in any other subject – but it is perhaps in the teaching of Modern Languages that the greatest emphasis is given to the learning and building up of these skills.

In the National Curriculum for England, teachers of Modern Languages are encouraged to make links with other subjects and parents might also look for opportunities to do the same. In fact, parents can sometimes be ideally placed to take advantage of opportunities that arise to use the language, to respond to cultural aspects around them and indeed to exploit the all important fun element of language learning. In those families that are already bilingual, the foreign language being learnt may in fact be the third language and this might provide opportunities for points of comparison. Some areas for exploitation could include:

- aspects of mathematics, such as counting, handling money, telling the time, saying the date;
- using information technology to look up information on the Internet about festivals or summer activities in the country or communicate with friends abroad through e-mail;
- research into the history and geography of the country or place where the foreign language is spoken, prior to going on holiday;
- learning or simply enjoying songs, stories and poems.

what parents say ...

My son learnt French in a fun way at junior school and it definitely helped him to have a positive attitude to learning a language when he got to secondary school. I think we in Britain are a bit complacent when it comes to learning languages, so I think it's great that children are turned on to it as early as possible.

(Parent of Joe, 13)

three

What is being taught?

As you have read in the previous chapter, the development of language teaching in primary schools has varied across the country and, in the absence of any prescribed schemes of work, schools or local authorities have inevitably created their own. Despite this situation there are common threads running through these schemes of work, partly because there are obvious starting points and partly because of the work done through in-service training, conferences, and publications by CILT.

The most commonly taught language, for a number of reasons, is French. Teachers in primary schools are much more likely to have some knowledge of, and confidence in, their ability to speak and work with the French language. As our nearest neighbour, it is also more feasible for schools to consider visits or exchanges than would be possible with Spain or Italy, for example. Other languages may be taught – in particular Spanish, German or Italian, and in some schools the focus is on language awareness rather than proficiency in one particular language. In such cases shorter blocks of work on a number of different languages may be provided.

Most schools will tend to start with everyday conversational language: greetings, introductions and the words necessary to talk about oneself and ask questions of others. The programme may follow a series of topics – those suggested in the QCA scheme of work for Key Stage 2 are reflected in the strands that are commonly found in primary teaching (as shown right).

1	I speak French/Spanish/German
2	About me
3	My family
4	Animals
5	My birthday
6	The world
7	Me and my school
8	What would you like?
9	Sport
10	Clothes
11	I live in …
12	A French-speaking country

Children will learn to listen to and understand simple expressions in the language, and also to express themselves orally with increasing confidence and accuracy. They will be learning new vocabulary items not in isolation as words in a list, but to use in the context of simple sentence structures in order to communicate with others. For example, parents may notice that verbs are not chanted in the way they may have done at school. Meaning and communication are paramount so verb forms will be learnt in the context of a particular expression.

As in the QCA scheme of work, the curriculum may have aspects designed to help children to understand and appreciate the culture of the country as well as its language.

what parents say …

When we were at the campsite in France I heard Matt say _'J'ai deux sœurs, Annie et Chloe – et toi?'._ The phrases they had learnt about talking about themselves sounded so natural and were a really good way in to getting to know French kids. They got a real buzz from being able to make themselves understood!

(Parent of Matthew, 9)

four

How are foreign languages taught in primary schools?

As with what is being taught (see Chapter 3), actual practice may vary, but a broadly similar picture will be seen in most schools.

It is unlikely that a great deal of time will be allocated within the timetable – somewhere between 30 minutes and an hour would seem to be fairly typical. In many schools this is topped up by use of the language throughout the school week, for example in calling and answering the register, in writing the date, or recording the weather.

Work within the language lessons will be predominantly focused on listening and speaking, with writing and reading activities being introduced with older juniors. A variety of approaches may be used to introduce new language to children – this may include use of flashcards, video programmes, puppets, games and cassette recordings of native speakers. Related activities to give children the opportunity to practise what they have learnt, may take place in smaller groups and include a whole variety of games, role play, songs, surveys and use of the computer. At this stage children will be encouraged not just to repeat the same structures they have learnt, but also to begin to use those structures to construct their own simple sentences and expressions.

Depending on their own ability and confidence, teachers may conduct all, or nearly all, of the lesson in the target language. Although this can be daunting to children at first, by using carefully chosen phrases and backing them up with gestures and mime, it is possible to create a climate where children can follow what is being said and enjoy the challenge of 'solving the puzzle'. While obviously helping them to develop their listening skills, it also demonstrates the language in action, ensuring that they experience it as more than just a series of exercises and games.

In some schools, children may be lucky enough to work with native speakers of the language. This adds another dimension to children's learning, not just in terms of authentic accent and cultural understanding, but also an appreciation of the reality of the living language – and their ability to use what they have learnt to communicate successfully to somebody from another country.

Much of what is described above is encapsulated in the following excerpt from the 'Policy for teaching French' which a London junior school has produced. Parents wanting to support their children's language learning at home may like to ask to see their school's policy document, if there is one, to ensure that their home approach complements and builds on that of the school.

aims	

- To encourage positive attitudes to the learning of a foreign language and a sympathetic approach to other cultures.
- To increase children's understanding of the way languages work.
- To develop children's ability, confidence and enjoyment in communicating in the French language.
- To increase children's awareness of France and its culture.
- To promote the personal and social development of the child through encouraging children to work co-operatively, experience success and gain enhanced self-esteem.
- To develop children's ability to listen attentively and to speak with confidence.

approach	

- We use a communicative approach, in which all children can actively engage in meaningful tasks and where the target language is exploited as much as possible.
- Greatest emphasis is given to listening and speaking, with reading and some writing where appropriate.
- Tasks and activities will: have clear, achievable objectives;
  be carefully planned and structured;
  be practical, active and varied;
  include small group and paired work;
  promote success and self-esteem.
- French is taught in a session of approximately 30–40 minutes per week, but with incidental use of the language where possible.
- Opportunities will be sought for children to work with people whose first language is French (for example, assistants, parents, visitors).

Excerpt from policy of Trafalgar Junior School, Twickenham

what parents say ...

I think that the key point for us is to 'make it fun'. In my experience, as soon as children feel that they must learn something difficult, their enthusiasm can evaporate and they can see it as a chore. Using games and songs is a sure-fire way to keep the interests of my children!

(Parent of Megan, 9, and Chris, 6)

part two

Practical activities to do with your child

five
Helping your child get started

Your starting point will depend on a number of factors, including the age of the child, their interests, any existing knowledge of the language they may have and your own linguistic capability.

It is important that children should not be faced with tasks that are too challenging in the early stages as this may be discouraging. The best starting points are activities that are easy to succeed at and fun in themselves, with a focus on listening and speaking.

For younger children, songs and rhymes are a good way in as they offer the opportunity to play while getting used to the 'music' and sounds of the language concerned. In these very early stages, simply integrating the use of the daily language into daily life and playing a few games can provide a gentle, accessible start.

For older children and those with some knowledge of the language being learnt, computer-based activities may prove a motivating and enjoyable starting point. It is important in the early stages to ensure that the spoken language is introduced alongside or before the written form.

The Internet can bring a wealth of learning opportunities direct from the country concerned into your home. It is important to be selective about the websites you use; many which are designed for much younger children will be appropriate for the older early language learner. Suggestions for finding resources and sites are given throughout the book, but of course new ones are always appearing and creative use of search engines from the country concerned (e.g. **fr.yahoo.com, es.yahoo.com, de.yahoo.com**) will give many more.

If you have a holiday planned to the country, not only will motivation to learn be strong, but the many opportunities for real communicative use of the target language, however simple, can show what a relevant and exciting activity language learning is. It is important to remember that a light touch is needed to prevent a family holiday becoming an off-putting homework activity!

As with many learning situations, ringing the changes can help to maintain interest and enthusiasm and dipping into the different chapters should enable you to do this. At the same time, it may be clear that your child particularly enjoys, and learns from, a certain kind of activity or approach, and this should be taken advantage of.

Songs and rhymes were a good place to start and they quickly became part of the repertoire. Then we looked at the Internet to find more songs and found masses of good sites which really kept the children's interest going.

(Parent of Alex, 8)

Rhymes, songs and poems

Parents of young children will have had lots of experience developing their child's listening and speaking skills since babyhood using:

- nursery rhymes;
- finger rhymes;
- nonsense songs;
- traditional songs.

To many, this is such a natural part of playing with their child that they may not have really stopped to think much about it. These songs and rhymes from childhood are often simple, repetitive and fun. It is because of this that they are easy to remember and establish a pattern or rhythm in our heads. The same applies to songs and rhymes in a foreign language. Adults often remember songs that they learned at school long after other aspects of the foreign language have disappeared.

Many of the songs and rhymes we use with our children are familiar to us from our own childhood, others are picked up from television and other media. Unless you were brought up or have lived in a country where the foreign language is spoken, it is unlikely that you will have that core of material at your fingertips. If this is the case, this chapter offers some songs and rhymes to get you started and recommends some resources that are available for purchase or might be found in a library.

Simple songs and rhymes

Finger rhymes or games are an enjoyable way of learning and practising sounds, words and phrases in a foreign language. The actual physical stimulus of using their fingers and hands does, of course, help children to remember the new words. It is a good idea to introduce new rhymes gradually, one by one, to avoid confusion.

La Jolie Ronde Ltd produces a useful source of ideas for finger rhymes in French. The video *Jeux de Doigts* demonstrates some simple rhymes and actions. This is also a good resource if you need help with your own pronunciation.

A simple finger rhyme to start with if your child is new to learning French is taken from *Jeux de Doigts* as above, although you could of course, adapt it for a different language:

Les escargots	**The snails**
Deux petits escargots dans le jardin.	Two little snails in the garden.
Bonjour. Bonjour!	Hello. Hello!

This most basic of finger rhymes can build up into a longer one:

Il pleut	**It's raining**
Deux petits escargots.	Two little snails.
Bonjour. Bonjour!	Hello. Hello!
Comment ça va?	How are you?
Ça va bien merci – et toi?	Very well, thank you – and you?
Non, ça ne va pas – il pleut.	Not very well – it's raining.
Je rentre chez moi.	I'm going home.

You can make up appropriate actions and of course, elaborate even further by using finger puppets or drawings, imagining that the two snails are having a conversation.

Some finger rhymes already familiar to children in English, such as 'Round and round the garden' also have their foreign language equivalents, such as:

Une petite bête	**One little creature**
Une petite bête ...	One little creature …
Qui monte, qui monte, qui monte ...	which climbs up, and up, and up …
Et qui fait guili-guili.	and tickles you under there.

There is a wealth of nursery rhymes often set to traditional tunes that can be chanted as you climb the stairs or sung during a car journey. Although the meaning may be absolute nonsense, they provide rhythm and rhyme and can reinforce new language in a fun way, for example, numbers:

Un deux trois	**One two three**
Un deux trois	One two three
Allons dans les bois.	Let's go to the woods.
Quatre cinq six	Four five six
Cueillir des cerises.	To pick some cherries.
Sept huit neuf	Seven eight nine
Dans mon panier neuf.	In my new basket.
Dix onze douze	Ten eleven twelve
Elles seront toutes rouges.	They will all be red.

Or parts of the body, using mime or a doll:

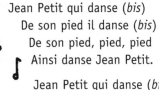

Jean Petit qui danse	**John Small is dancing**
Jean Petit qui danse (*bis*)	John Small is dancing (*repeat*)
De son pied il danse (*bis*)	With his foot he's dancing (*repeat*)
De son pied, pied, pied	With his foot, foot, foot
Ainsi danse Jean Petit.	So John Small is dancing.
Jean Petit qui danse (*bis*)	John Small is dancing (*repeat*)
De sa tête il danse (*bis*)	With his head he's dancing (*repeat*)
De sa tête, tête, tête	With his head, head, head
De son pied, pied, pied	With his foot, foot, foot
Ainsi danse Jean Petit.	So John Small is dancing.

With each verse, you can add a different part of the body, moving your body or a doll to indicate the part of the body:

de son cou	with his neck
de sa main	with his hand
de son doigt	with his finger
de son coude	with his elbow
de son genou.	with his knee.

Or clothes, pointing to the relevant items as they are mentioned, presenting them dramatically and miming putting them on to build up suspense and increase the fun:

Promenons-nous dans les bois	**Let's walk in the woods**
Promenons-nous dans les bois	Let's walk in the woods
Pendant que le loup n'y est pas.	While the wolf isn't there.
Si le loup y était	If the wolf was there
Il nous mangerait.	He would eat us.
Mais comme il n'y est pas	But as he isn't there
Il nous mangera pas.	He won't eat us.
Loup y-es-tu?	Wolf, are you there?
Que fais-tu?	What are you doing?
(the wolf replies while getting dressed)	
Je mets ma chemise!	I'm putting on my shirt!

After repeating the chorus each time, you can add on a new item of clothing, such as:

Je mets mes chaussures ...	I'm putting on my shoes ...
Je mets ma veste ...	I'm putting on my jacket ...
Je mets mes chaussettes ...	I'm putting on my socks ...
Je mets ma cravate ...	I'm putting on my tie ...
Je mets mes lunettes ...	I'm putting on my glasses ...
Je mets mon chapeau ...	I'm putting on my hat ...

A short, simple German song about clothes, in which repetition increases children's familiarity with sounds and words:

Mein Hut der hat drei Ecken	**My hat it has three corners**
Mein Hut der hat drei Ecken	My hat it has three corners
Drei Ecken hat mein Hut	Three corners has my hat
Und hätt' er nicht drei Ecken	And had it not three corners
Dann wär'st auch nicht mein Hut.	It would not be my hat.

Another song in German gives the opportunity to mime the actions, add more verses and practise the colours:

Grün, grün, grün sind alle meine Kleider	**Green, green, green are all my clothes**
Grün, grün, grün sind alle meine Kleider	Green, green, green are all my clothes
Grün, grün, grün ist alles, was ich hab!	Green, green, green is all I have!
Darum lieb ich alles, was so grün ist,	But I love everything that's green,
Weil mein Schatz ein Jäger ist.	Because my darling is a hunter.
Blau, blau, blau sind alle meine Kleider	Blue, blue, blue are all my clothes
Blau, blau, blau ist alles, was ich hab!	Blue, blue, blue is all I have!
Darum lieb ich alles, was so blau ist,	But I love everything that's blue,
Weil mein Schatz eine Matrose ist.	Because my darling is a sailor.

This is an example of a song where once your child has learnt a verse, you can add more colours and occupations. Thus:

Rot + ein Reiter	red + rider
Weiss + ein Bäcker	white + baker
Schwarz + ein Schornsteinfeger	black + chimney sweep
Bunt + ein Maler	colourful + painter.

Some songs and rhymes are just fun to say and to get your tongue around, for example:

Il pleut, il mouille	**It's raining, it's wet**
Il pleut, il mouille,	It's raining, it's wet,
La grenouille est à l'abri	The frog is taking shelter
Dessous un grand parapluie.	Under a big umbrella.

Traditional songs

Traditional songs can be quite difficult to understand, due to the language and context sometimes being old fashioned. However, they are an important part of the culture of the country and can be fun to sing. The French publisher, Casterman, has a series of books in which traditional songs are broken down line by line, in picture story format, and can be sung, or read aloud if you don't know the tune.

If you want to sing some songs with your child, you will find it useful to listen to them on a cassette or CD, first. This will ensure that you are clear about the pronunciation! You can often find collections of children's songs in hypermarkets abroad or via the relevant Amazon website (see p30 for details). Singers to look out for include Rosa Leon for Spanish, Detlev Jöcker for German and Henri Dès, French. You can also find inexpensive collections of traditional children's songs. One tip however – make sure that you buy a version that comes with the words printed out. Websites such as those listed at the end of the chapter provide lyrics and tunes for a wide range of suitable songs.

Alphabet songs are easy to find and fun to sing. We have provided French, German and Spanish alphabet pronunciation guides in the appendix. Here is an example from Detlev Jöcker:

Das ABC-Lied	The ABC song

A B C D E F G	A B C D E F G
Ach, mir tut der Bauch so weh!	Oh, I have such stomach ache!
Bauch so weh!	Such stomach ache!
H I J K L M N O P	H I J K L M N O P
Ich koche mir eine Tasse Tee.	I'm making myself a cup of tea.
Tasse Tee.	Cup of tea.
Q R S T U V W	Q R S T U V W
Die trinke ich langsam aus und geh.	I drink it up slowly and go.
Aus und geh.	Up and go.
X Ypsilon Z	X Y Z
Schnell in mein weiches warmes Bett.	Quickly to my wide, warm bed.
Warmes Bett.	Warm bed.

Another simple alphabet rhyme in German:

A B C, die Katze lief im Schnee	A B C, the cat ran in the snow

A B C, die Katze lief im Schnee	A B C, the cat ran in the snow
Und als sie dann nach Hause kam,	And when she came home,
Da hatt' sie weisse Stiefel an.	She had white boots on.
A B C, die Katze lief im Schnee.	A B C, the can ran in the snow.

A French alphabet rhyme:

L'alphabet	The alphabet

A, B, C, D, le chat s'est décidé	A, B, C, D, the cat decided
E, F, G, H, à saisir une hache	E, F, G, H, to take an axe
I, J, K, L, pour couper la ficelle	I, J, K, L, to cut the string

M, N, O, P, où le jambon salé
Q, R, S, T, est pendu tout l'été.
U, V, W, le jambon est tombé
X, Y, Z, tout juste sur sa tête.
Le voici étourdi
Et nous avons le temps
De redire à présent
Notre alphabet sans lui.

M, N, O, P, where the salted ham
Q, R, S, T, hung all summer.
U, V, W, the ham fell
X,Y,Z, right on his head.
Here he is, knocked out
And now we have the time
to say again
Our alphabet, without him.

A, B, C, D, E, F, G, H, I, J, K, L, M, N, O, P, Q, R, S, T, U, V, W, X, Y, Z.

Well-known songs

Even if your own repertoire of songs in the foreign language that your child is learning is limited, you will find that some at least, have a familiar tune, such as the 'Happy Birthday' song:

French

Joyeux anniversaire
Joyeux anniversaire
Joyeux anniversaire
Joyeux anniversaire (*name*)
Joyeux anniversaire!

German

Zum Geburtstag viel Glück
Zum Geburtstag viel Glück
Zum Geburtstag viel Glück
Zum Geburtstag liebe (*girl's name*)/lieber (*boy's name*)
Zum Geburtstag viel Glück!

Italian

Tanti auguri a te
Tanti auguri a te
Tanti auguri a te
Tanti auguri a (*name*)
Tanti auguri a te!

Spanish

Cumpleaños feliz
Cumpleaños feliz
Cumpleaños feliz
Te deseamos todos
¡Cumpleaños feliz!

Another example of a song that translates easily into many languages is *'Frère Jacques'*. Here are some versions to help you:

French	*German*	*Italian*	*Spanish*
Frère Jacques	**Bruder Jakob**	**Frà Martino**	**Fray Felipe**
Frère Jacques,	Bruder Jakob,	Frà Martino,	Fray Felipe,
Frère Jacques,	Bruder Jakob,	campanaro,	Fray Felipe,
Dormez-vous?	Schläfst du noch?	Dormi tu?	¿Duermes tu?
Dormez-vous?	Schläfst du noch?	Dormi tu?	¿Duermes tu?
Sonnez les matines!	Hörst du nicht die	Suona le campane!	¡Toca la campana!
Sonnez les matines!	Glocken?	Suona le campane!	¡Toca la campana!
Ding dang dong,	Hörst du nicht die	Din don dan,	Tin ton tin,
Ding dang dong!	Glocken?	Din don dan.	Tin ton tin.
	Ding dang dong,		
	Ding dang dong.		

Look out also for nursery rhymes that will be familiar to your child in English, such as 'Hickory dickory dock':

Tickedi tickedi tack

Tickedi tickedi tack,
Die Maus läuft die Uhr auf und ab.
Die Uhr schlät eins,
Die Maus rennt heim.
Tickedi tickedi tack!

'Twinkle twinkle little star' is another song that has a German equivalent:

Funkle, funkle, kleiner Stern

Funkle, funkle, kleiner Stern
Was du bist, das wüsst ich gern.
Stehst hoch über aller Welt
Ein Diamand am Himmelszeit.
Funkle, funkle, kleiner Stern
Was du bist das wüsst ich gern.

A French Christmas song is sung to the tune of 'Jingle bells':

Vive le vent

Vive le vent (*repeat*)
Vive le vent d'hiver,
Qui s'en va, tout en soufflant
Dans les grands sapins verts.
Oh! Vive le vent (*repeat*)
Vive le vent d'hiver,
Boule de neige et jour de l'An
Et bonne année grand-mère!

what parents say ...

Watching videos and learning songs is definitely a good way of picking up the language. Children seem to learn and remember songs much quicker than adults and don't realise that they are learning. My children are still singing a song that they learnt eight weeks ago!

(Parent of Megan, 9, and Chris, 6)

i

books | French

Kyprianou, M. *Il était une bergère.* Casterman (ISBN 2-203-13431-3).

Moulou, P. *Le livre d'or de la chanson traditionnelle française.* Marabout (ISBN 2-501-01842-7).

video | French

Jeux de Doigts. La Jolie Ronde Ltd (**www.lajolieronde.co.uk**).

La Jolie Ronde is an early years publisher and organiser of after-school French classes for primary children.

songs | spanish

Leon, R. *Los cochinitos.* Fonomusic (8 423479 041824).

websites | French

www.pouletfrites.com
A fun website for children (2–5 years), with interactive games. Useful for parents and teachers.

www.momes.net
An international website for young French speakers. A good source for nursery rhymes and poems for parents and teachers.

www.bonjour.org.uk
Contains activities for children, such as presentation of vocabulary + sound.

www.paroles.net
Lyrics of French songs (including pop) with music.

www.bonjour.com
Free French lessons to refresh your own language skills, whether parent or teacher.

websites | German

www.sprachhexen.com
A source of information on books in German, arranged by age group (5–14 years).

www.hallo.org.uk
Takes you straight to the German resources (books, videos and DVDs) on Amazon, with rubric in English.

websites | Spanish

www.hola.org.uk
Quick links to the Spanish resources (books, videos and DVDs) section on Amazon, with rubric in English.

websites | multilingual

www.linguatots.com
Suitable for parents with little or no knowledge of French, German, Italian and Spanish. Gives a parents' guide of how to start helping your child and recommends products for babies, toddlers, pre-school and primary.

www.laukart.de
Children's songs and rhymes in more than twenty languages, including Cantonese, Japanese and Korean. Useful for parents bringing up children bilingually, if your language is represented.

www.bilingual-supplies.co.uk
Books for children aged 2–12 years, includes minority languages and English as an additional language.

www.georgetown.edu/ cball/animals
Useful for developing awareness of language, sounds of the world's animals, in languages from Albanian to Vietnamese.

further reading

Martin, C. ResourceFile 6: *Rhythm and rhyme.* CILT. A good source of simple songs and rhymes in French and German, with supporting activities.

Cheater, C. and Martin, C. Young Pathfinder 6: *Let's join in!* CILT. Ideas for teachers and parents for rhymes, poems and songs.

resources

seven

Using games

In the early stages of language learning, motivation and fun are crucial. Games can provide opportunities for children to learn in an active way, with enjoyment and social interaction a necessary part of the process.

The number games that follow will teach counting but will also introduce other vocabulary and simple structures as well as familiarising children with the sounds of the language. Many of the suggested activities in the word games section can be easily adapted to teach any vocabulary.

Number games

COUNTING RHYMES

Make up your own simple counting rhymes to use as skipping or clapping rhymes:

Un, deux, trois
Ooh, la, la.
Quatre, cinq, six
Les cerises.
Sept, huit, neuf
Un grand bœuf.

Or use common French, German and Spanish counting rhymes:

French   Un, deux, trois, quatre, cinq, six, sept
T'es une omelette.
Un, deux, trois, quatre, cinq, six, sept

Violette, Violette.
Un, deux, trois, quatre, cinq, six, sept
Violette à bicyclette.

German Eins, zwei – Polizei
Drei, vier – Offizier
Fünf, sechs – alte Hex
Sieben, acht – gute Nacht
Neun, zehn – auf Wiedersehen.

Spanish En la casa de Pinocho
Todos cuentan hasta ocho.
Uno, dos, tres, cuatro,
Cinco, seis, siete, ocho.

'Ten in the bed'

Take a well known song such as 'Ten in the bed' and adapt it in the foreign language, for example:

Dix au lit et le petit dit	Ten in the bed and the little one said
Poussez-vous, poussez-vous!	Roll over, roll over!
Neuf au lit et le petit dit	Nine in the bed and the little one said
Poussez-vous, poussez-vous!	Roll over, roll over!

(Carry on with huit, sept, six, cinq, quatre, trois, *until:)*

Deux au lit et le petit dit	Two in the bed and the little one said
Pousse-toi, pousse-toi!	Roll over, roll over (*in the singular form*)!
Un au lit et le petit dit	One in the bed and the little one said
Bonne nuit! Bonne nuit!	Good night! Good night!

Counting in French

Substitute French numbers for English ones in ordinary counting situations: 'by the time I count to *dix* I want you tucked up in bed! *Un, deux …*'; counting out sweets, biscuits, etc; when counting moves in any dice game; counting out pocket money.

Dates

Work out the date in the language each day. If possible find a French calendar to refer to (see 'Resources' section at the end of this chapter).

OUT AND ABOUT/IN THE CAR

When out and about, say the numbers on car registration plates:

- as separate digits: *trois, deux, huit;*
- as separate digits and add them up: *trois plus deux plus huit font treize!;*
- as one big number: *trois cent vingt-huit.*

On a car journey, count the cars – each passenger chooses a colour (in the language, e.g. *rosso, azul, amarillo*). Then keep a count of cars with your colour. First to *diez* wins!

NUMBER 'HANGMAN'

Take it in turns to think of a number, sum, etc. Others have to guess a digit or a sign at a time. If they guess wrongly, another part of the hangman figure is drawn. For example, one person might think of: 3 + 12 = 15 *(trois plus douze fait quinze).* They draw out seven spaces to write in.

— — — — — — —

'FIZZ, BUZZ'

Take it in turns to count the next number. 'Fizz' is used in place of multiples of 3. 'Buzz' is used in place of multiples of 5. Start counting: *uno, dos,* fizz, *cuatro,* buzz, fizz, *siete, ocho,* fizz, buzz, *once,* fizz, *trece, catorce,* fizz buzz.

You can change what 'fizz' and 'buzz' stand for! This is good practice for simple mental maths skills as well as the language!

BINGO/*LOTO*

Play 'Bingo'/'Loto' in the language – take it in turns to be the caller.

PLAYING CARDS

Adapt games with playing cards so that it is necessary to say the numbers in the foreign language. For example, try 'Snap', where you can only keep the cards if you have said the numbers correctly in the language. Equally fun is 'Pelmanism' or pairs. All the cards are face down on the table. The object is to find pairs but you have to say the numbers correctly to keep them and win another go!

'DOMINOES'

Play with conventional dominoes, but to have your go you must say the numbers correctly, or make special dominoes which require the player to match the word with the number:

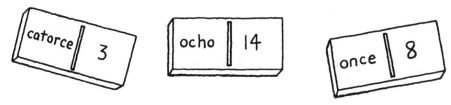

Word games

Many of the games suggested here can be adapted to teach, practise or reinforce any vocabulary.

'KIM'S GAME'

The basic idea of this game is that the player is given a short time to memorise a number of objects on a tray or table. The objects are removed and players then have to recall what was there. This is a game that can be used to reinforce vocabulary. Actual objects can be used – or pictures cut out of a magazine, for example of foods.

A variation is to remove one item when the player is not looking. Players then guess what it was.

'PELMANISM'/'PAIRS'

The same rules apply as when it is played with cards (see 'Playing cards' above, in 'Number games' section), but picture cards – or a combination of picture and word cards are used.

COLOURS

To reinforce colours, collect a number of items of different shapes and sizes, one for each colour learnt. Children can look at them for a given time and then, blindfolded, must identify the colour of each by its shape.

'HAPPY FAMILIES'

Try to buy a 'Happy families' pack if visiting the country – if not adapt an English language set. This is a good way to learn and practise family vocabulary.

LATERAL THINKING

Find connections between words. Children can really enjoy the sounds of words and appreciate common origins. It can help with memorising vocabulary and with awareness of spelling too – but beware of those words which seem similar, but have different meanings!

For example: *la lune* (moon) – *lundi* (Monday) ➤ lunar – lunatic

un (one) ➤ unique – unite – union

gracias (thanks) ➤ grateful – grace – gratitude

If you know any Latin, you can always introduce it to make further links! (e.g. *luna* is Latin for moon).

FORTUNE TELLERS

Make 'fortune tellers' using pictures, colours or words in the language. Children love making and playing with these and the game is good for young language learners as it requires an oral response!

After picking a particular number and colour, a secret message is revealed, for example: *Tu es méchant* or *Je t'aime.*

LISTENING

If two or more children are learning, you can play games which focus on listening skills and require a quick response. For example, after introducing some vocabulary, you can put picture or word cards (depending on what stage they are at) in front of them. Then tell a simple story containing them. When they hear the words represented by the card they must try to be the first to touch it.

INTERNET

You can find websites which contain interactive games requiring a response from the player (see 'Using the Internet' below).

OFF-THE-SHELF GAMES

Professionally produced games in foreign languages can be purchased from many of the suppliers listed in the 'Resources' section, including versions of well-known games such as 'Monopoly' and 'Cluedo'.

what parents say ...

I explained the word games to the children and asked them which ones they liked the sound of best. They liked Kim's Game and games where there was a bit of a competitive element, like the story activity where they had to try to be the first to touch a card. They love anything that makes them laugh – like silly number rhymes and *Ten in the bed*. I think the fact that it was fun will help them to remember the words.

(Parent of Megan, 9, and Chris, 6)

books | French

Chapouton, A. *Comptines pour jouer avec les sons.* Flammarion (ISBN 2-08-160088-9).

de Hoestland, J. *Cinq comptines pour s'endormir.* Flammarion (ISBN 2-08-163530-5).

Poésie, comptines et chansons pour le soir. Gallimard Jeunesse (ISBN 2-07-054707-8).

Three books that contain counting rhymes – the last also with CD.

books | Spanish

Budwell, N. *Cuenta con Clifford.* Mariposa (ISBN 0-59-087589-2).

Gibson, R. *Juegos con numeros.* Usborne (ISBN 0-74-603870-4).

Brusca, M. L. *Tres amigos.* H. Hill & Co (ISBN 0-80-503707-1).

Books with counting activities.

websites

For internet sites containing games and other activities see 'Using the Internet', p44.

A French calendar can be printed out from: **actu63.free.fr/calendrier_2003.htm**

further reading

Martin, C. Young Pathfinder 2: *Games and fun activities.* CILT.

resources

eight
Using books and other published material

There are many books published designed to help children in the early stages of language learning but these can often present problems, as the focus is usually on the written forms of the language. If children are left to work by themselves they are unlikely to learn the correct spoken forms. Activities presented in such books are often of a simple 'fill the gaps' format which can become uninteresting and does little to develop a child's use of language structures. Some such materials may have a place if used by the child with the support of an adult or as reinforcement of areas which have already been worked on.

Story books in the target language can provide great opportunities for enjoyable language development but, again, require the support of an adult with some proficiency in the language. Book and tape sets can provide the opportunity for parent and child to follow the story in the book, while hearing it read by a native speaker.

Choosing story books

Care must be taken in the choice of books. Whilst books written for younger children may appear too young in terms of interest level for the slightly older language learner, the simple structures, repetition, and limited vocabulary can make them ideal. In fact all children love picture books and even older ones can enjoy the opportunity – or the excuse! – to read them.

Many picture books published abroad are translations of English language books, and it can be a great bonus if the child is already familiar with the English text version. It is important, however, to be aware that good translations will not necessarily be completely literal, if comparing the two texts.

The main criteria for choosing a book in another language are:

- a limited amount of text;
- simple language structures;
- a combination of picture and text that is supportive to grasping
- the meaning;
- repetition of simple phrases or vocabulary;
- short enough to read at one sitting.

Some examples of appropriate books are given below, but the following excerpt from the text of *Une histoire sombre … très sombre* (published originally in English as *A dark, dark tale*, see 'Resources' section on p42) illustrates the point.

Il était une fois un pays sombre, très sombre.
Dans ce pays, il y avait un bois sombre, très sombre.
Dans ce bois, il y avait un château sombre, très sombre.
Devant ce château, il y avait une porte sombre, très sombre
Derrière cette porte, il y avait une salle sombre, très sombre.
Dans cette salle, il y avait un escalier sombre, très sombre.
En haut de cet escalier, il y avait un couloir sombre, très sombre.

Once upon a time there was a dark, dark moor.
On the moor there was a dark, dark wood.
In the wood there was a dark, dark house.
At the front of the house there was a dark, dark door.
Behind the door there was a dark, dark hall.
In the hall there were some dark, dark stairs.
Up the stairs there was a dark, dark passage.

How can I use a story book?

If the choice of book has been carefully made, then it should be possible in the first instance to let it speak for itself. Reading together so that the child can see the pictures, perhaps pointing to specific parts of the picture should enable the child to get the gist of the story, if not understand every word.

As with any early reader, discussion and repetition of what is being read is really important. It will not take many readings of the book before the child will be able to predict the beginning of the next sentence.

Although it would be possible to prepare the child by teaching some of the key vocabulary first (and this may be a good idea for some books), it is more satisfying for

the reader – and more likely to lead to memorable learning – if they have w
the meaning themselves using the clues available in the pictures and surround___

Once familiar with a book such as the above, it can be enjoyable to devise some activities based on it. For example:

- Can you remember the order of places mentioned in the book?
- Can we make our own simple book in the language, following a similar structure?
- What words for situation (adverbs) are used? (*dans, devant, derrière, en haut de*)

It is important not to overdo follow-up activities, as the pleasure of reading the book and understanding its language are the main objectives.

Dual language books, where the text is printed in both English and the foreign language are available, but may lead to too much focus on translation, rather than the meaning of the foreign language in its own right. One excellent example in English and French is the picture book *The tunnel/Le tunnel* by Brian Wildsmith which was written to celebrate the opening of the Channel Tunnel in Summer 1994. This amusing and beautifully illustrated book tells the story of two moles, one French and one English, who tunnel under the Channel to meet each other.

Some very attractively produced magazines and comics are published which, although they may be intended for younger native speakers, will have language which is appropriate for the early language learner. These are available from newsagents abroad, or by subscription. They can be posted to British addresses.

what parents say …

My children already knew *Not now Bernard* really well, so they had no difficulty in following what was going on. They loved the different sounds of the language and we've had to read it through with them several times. What I like about this approach is that it seems to make the children curious about how the language works and how the French version compares with the English one that they knew. It's also great that some of the sentences seem to have become catch phrases now – I heard Jonathan say *Pas maintenant, Katie*. It did surprise me how accessible books in another language can be if you choose the right ones! We will definitely try to get hold of more simple books in French.

(Parent of Katie, 7, and Jonathan, 9)

ℹ

Brown, R. *Une histoire sombre ... très sombre.* Folio Benjamin (ISBN 2-07-054811-2).

McKee, D. *Bernard et le monstre (Not now Bernard).* Folio Benjamin (ISBN 2-07-054882-1).

Ramos, M. *Maman!* Lutin Poche (ISBN 2-211-06061-7).

Maes, D. *Chapeau!* Magnard Jeunesse (ISBN 2-210-97930-7).

Gardiner, L. *Lola et Max.* Hachette (ISBN 2-01-390830.X).

Guettier, B. *Je m'habille et je te croque.* Lutin Poche (ISBN 2-211-105597-4).

Carle, E. *La chenille qui fait des trous (The very hungry caterpillar).* Mijade Album (ISBN 2-87-143-1366).

Wildsmith, B. *The tunnel/Le tunnel.* OUP (ISBN 0-19-279962-2).

books | German

Pfister, M. *Der Regenbogenfisch (The rainbowfish).* North South Books (ISBN 3-31401173-3).

> There will be many books which fulfil the criteria described in this chapter. The books listed here may provide a good starting point.

books | Spanish

Sendak, M. *Donde viven los monstruos (Where the wild things are).* Rayo (ISBN 0-06443422-2).

Emburley, R. *My day/Mi día.* Little Brown & Co.(ISBN 0-31-622983-0).

Emburley. R. *Let's go/Vamos.* Little Brown & Co. (ISBN 0-31-6230332).

publishers' websites

resources

www.amazon.fr and **www.amazon.de** Excellent sites for buying French and German books respectively. They display the front cover and a synopsis, and offer discounts and speedy dispatch.

www.grantandcutler.com The website of the largest foreign-language bookseller in the country. It has books, cassettes, CDs, videos and games in stock in many languages, including French Spanish, German, Italian and Portuguese.

www.younglinguists.com The website of European Schoolbooks Ltd. It sells a range of books, videos, cassettes, CDs and games.

other sources

Mantra Lingua
5 Alexandra Gve
London N12 8NU
Tel: 020 8445 5123
Mail order – specialists in dual language books.

Grant and Cutler
55–57 Great Marlborough Street
London W1F 7AY
Tel: 020 7734 2012
Foreign language bookshop (see above). They produce a catalogue and will accept orders by letter, fax telephone or e-mail.

European Schoolbooks
The Runnings
Cheltenham GL51 9PQ
Tel: 01242 245252
It produces a catalogue 'Languages for younger learners 5–15' and will accept orders by phone, fax, post or e-mail. It has the following retail outlets:

> **European Bookshop**
> **5 Warwick Street**
> **London W1B 5LU**
> **Tel: 020 7734 5259**
> Books in French, German, Spanish and Portuguese.

> **Italian Bookshop**
> **7 Cecil Court**
> **London WC2N 4EZ**
> **Tel: 020 7240 1634**

> **Young Europeans Bookstore**
> **5 Cecil Court**
> **London WC2N 4EZ**
> **Tel: 020 7836 6669**

www.milanpresse.com
The magazine *Petites Mains* is published by Milan Presse and available in newsagents in France or by subscription. Milan Presse produce a range of magazines for different ages which include stories, articles, puzzles and art and craft activities. To see the full range of Milan Presse publications, visit their website at **www.milanpresse.com.** Subscriptions can be accepted from the UK but an extra payment is required to cover postage.

resources

nine

Using the Internet

Using the Internet will not only help your child learn a foreign language but will also provide them with an interesting and authentic diet of stimulus material and also have the advantage of developing their information technology skills!

Throughout this book we have made references to show how the Internet can help you support your child's foreign language learning. In this chapter we aim to give some idea of the wealth of material available through the Internet.

Even if you do not have ready access at home or work, you can go on the Internet often free of charge at a public library. It helps to have an idea of what you are looking for so that you don't waste time. It's also a good idea to bookmark favourite websites so that you can return to them. Most are updated regularly and are worth revisiting from time to time. You may find it easier to start by 'surfing' until you find a couple of websites that you like and get used to. Then just get into the habit of checking them out as and when you need new material.

Some specific areas to look for on the Internet include:

- travel timetables and other travel information;
- weather forecasts;
- recipes;
- information about a particular place;
- school websites;
- specific hobbies and interests;
- songs, stories and jokes.

With a little time spent on research, perhaps together with your child, you will soon find sites to suit your interests and needs.

If you are looking for resources for children being brought up **bilingually,** there are many websites to help. At the end of the chapter, we list a small selection and these in turn will give you further useful links.

Songs

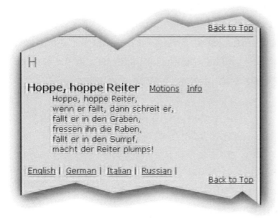

A website that offers a multilingual song book in languages that include Cantonese, Finnish, Indonesian, Norwegian and Vietnamese, in addition to those that your child might be learning at school. There is also an Esperanto section. The songs are arranged in themes and you can access the words for printing and also click to hear the music.

Where translations are available in alternative languages, there is a direct link to take you there.

Interactive games

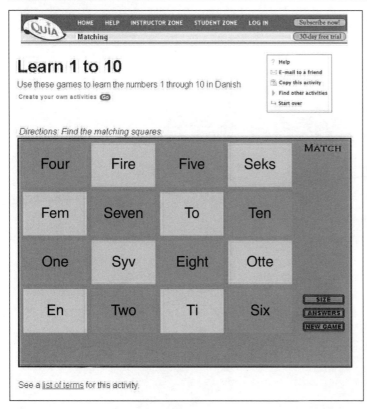

This has a range of activities in a variety of languages that might be useful if you were preparing to travel to a country where your child does not speak the language at all. This example for Danish provides an interactive game to learn the numbers 1–10. You could of course have fun in learning this alongside your child!

Produced for children, by children

A useful website for parents and teachers alike. This has a huge section of rhymes, songs and poems, again arranged under themes such as 'animals'. In this case it is possible with some items to print out an illustrated version. Look out for websites such as this – where all of the instructions and incidental language are in the target language – if you would like to expose your child to such semi-specialist terms as:

haut de la page	top of the page
version illustrée à imprimer	print illustrated version.

The above website also offers the example of a great way to access some simple stories, often created by children for children. With careful selection to contain enough key words that your child will understand, they can be used for reading aloud, learning off by heart or as a stimulus for a painting.

J'ai vu un dinosaure

Hier soir,
Je faisais mes devoirs
Quand j'ai vu un dinosaure
Glisser sous le canapé.
"Maman ! J'ai crié,
Y a un dinosaure!"
"Mais non, mon petit,
ce n'est que ton petit frère"

Cette nuit,
Je me suis endormi
Quand j'ai vu un dinosaure
Voler au milieu mon rêve.
"Maman ! J'ai crié,
Y a un dinosaure!"
"Mais non, mon petit,
ce n'est qu'un mouton sautant les barrières"

Ce matin,
J'ai pris mon bain
Quand j'ai vu un dinosaure
Nager sous la mousse.
"Maman ! J'ai crié,
Y a un dinosaure ! "
"Mais non, mon petit,
ce n'est que ta baleine en plastique"

Mais à quatre heures,
Je cherchais mon p'tit beurre,
Quand j'ai vu le dinosaure
Caché au fond de mon cartable.
Cette fois je n'ai pas crié.

Marie-Hélène Lafond

MOMES.NET

Traditional songs and stories

This is an excellent website for parents and teachers alike. This example of the song *'Le fermier dans son pré'* (the equivalent of 'The farmer in his den') enables you to click to hear the song – useful if you don't know or have forgotten the tune!

Although the example in French below of 'Little red riding hood' is somewhat lengthy and comes without pictures, you can still use it with your child. For example, if you wanted to do a well-known story with your child but do not have enough command of the foreign language to translate it yourself, you can chop up the text into segments and stick them on the back of illustrations cut up from a cheap version of the book or cover up the English text.

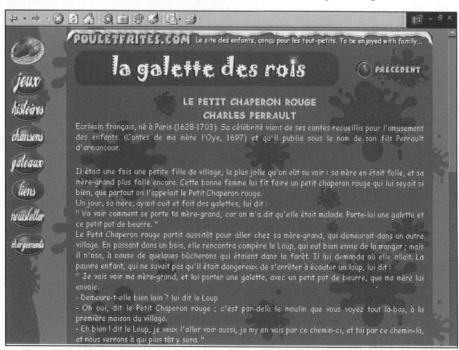

There is an obvious appeal to using a website like this that is written specifically for children and there are sometimes opportunities for more interactive use. This will be of particular interest if your child has reached the stage where they are ready to respond to the written word. A really simple example is from the list of birthdays that is updated every month. Your child could select someone who perhaps shares a birthday with them, click on their name and write a simple message. They may even get a reply in return! Equally, they have the opportunity to register their own birthday and wait for any greetings to arrive in the mail box.

Aujourd'hui Vendredi 2 Août 2002 c'est l'anniversaire de

- Michael (02/08/96)
- Michaël (02/08/95)
- Audrey (02/08/95)
- Cathy (02/08/95)
- Sonia (02/08/94)
- Eve (02/08/89)
- Jessica (02/08/89)
- Sahar (02/08/88)
- Quentin (02/08/88)
- Céline (02/08/88)
- Cristian (02/08/88)
- Angele (02/08/88)
- Andréa (02/08/86)
- Greégoire (02/08/85)
- Marie (02/08/84)
- Frédéric (02/08/84)
- Bélinda (02/08/83)
- Élodie (02/08/83)
- Heba (02/08/82)
- Louise (02/08/0)

n'oubliez pas de leur écrire.

Vous voulez qu'on vous souhaite votre anniversaire? Inscrivez-vous ici.

| 1 | 2 | 3 | 4 | 5 | 6 | 7 | 8 | 9 | 10 | 11 | 12 | 13 | 14 | 15 | 16 | 17 | 18 | 19 | 20 | 21 | 22 | 23 | 24 | 25 | 26 | 27 | 28 | 29 | 30 | 31 |
| Janvier | Février | Mars | Avril | Mai | Juin | Juillet | Août | Septembre | Octobre | Novembre | Décembre |

info@momes.net - © momes.net - 2001

Personal websites

Having considered the possibility of using material such as that found at **www.momes.net,** you may like to seek out some examples of children's own websites. Illustrated here is an example from an 11 year-old French boy. By clicking on the links, you can find out his personal profile, his heroes and links to other recommended sites. You might want to print this off for reading. In examples such as this, there is often also the possibility of clicking on an area that leads you directly into an e-mail reply. If you felt it suitable, your child could of course send off a response.

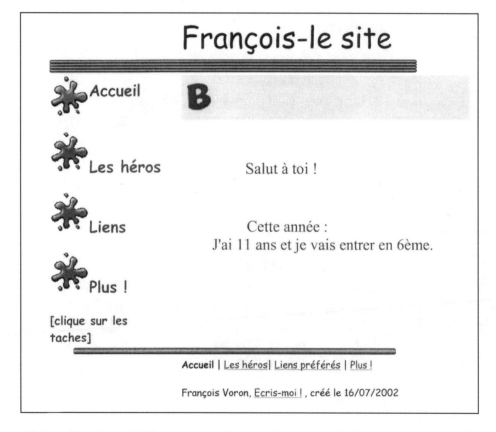

Along with a host of different types of material, you can also find recipes, often with simple illustrations or linked to special festivals. It can be fun to work out the ingredients needed, the instructions (the verbs at least are often very repetitive) and then have a go at preparing the dish.

Sending back an e-mail message

Again, this example from **www.momes.net** gives the opportunity of sending back a message to the person who registered the recipe.

Brochette de fruits

une recette proposée par
Brigitte
février 1999

ingrédients:

- Sections d'oranges

- Raisins verts ou rouges

- Cubes d'ananas

- Morceaux de cantaloup ou melon (le cantaloup c'est un gros melon, plus petit qu'une pastèque par exemple!, avec de la chair orangée à l'intérieur)
 ou

- Morceaux de pommes non-pelées ou bananes badigeonnées de citron, cerises, kiwis

Préparation:

- Alterner les morceaux de fruits sur des brochettes de bois ou des cure-dents...

Bon appétit!!

Seeking tourist information

Tourist information is easily obtainable and you might like to start by using one of the general search engines and just typing in the name of the place that you are interested in. Bear in mind however that this type of information is not necessarily written for children and you might need to hunt around to find material that will be simple enough at least to get the gist.

The following example from the town of Saint Romain in France has headings to click on. These are fairly standard and it might be useful for you to familiarise yourself with the type of information that they would reveal.

You can find photos of buildings and places in key French towns through accessing **www.pagesjaunes.fr/pj.cgi.** This is useful for giving children a flavour of French culture and showing them key monuments and tourist attractions.

what parents say …

David loves using the computer so it was a really good way in for him. He was really interested in the games – of course – but he liked the sites on www.momes.net and found a lad who loves the same things as him – computers, football, etc. I thought this was really good as it gave him more understanding of how children in other countries aren't necessarily so different. It also gave him a reason for trying to understand French!

(Parent of David, 11)

websites | French

www.infojunior.com
A great source of non-fiction reading material, includes sections on sport, animals and travel.

websites | German

www.spielstrasse.de
Puzzles, games and links to zoos.

www.kidsweb.de
Includes cookery, quizzes and art & craft activities.

websites | Italian

www.filastrocche.it
Includes poems, songs and links to e-pals.

www.lagirandola.it
Includes festivals, weather forecasts and useful links to other children's sites.

www.naturalia.org/ZOO/index.html
Information about and photos of animals from around the world.

websites |Spanish

www.pequenet.com
In the form of a children's newspaper, geared to the very young but accessible to all ages.

information for bilingual families

www.laukart.de
The multilingual families webring connects families who are raising their children in more than one language.

www.anacleta.homestead.com
Spanish and world language/culture links for children and their parents. Includes links to sites from which games and other products can be ordered.

www.bilingos.com
A collection of information for families where more than one language is being used. Gives links to further reading and information.

www.geocities.com/mhfurgason/lessons.html
Lessons, songs and games to teach your child as young as 18 months, in German and Spanish.

resources

ten

In town (at home and abroad)

Using the local environment for language learning, both at home and abroad, adds a motivating and fun dimension that is hard for schools to provide and is clearly a long way from a traditional homework activity. It also links the learning of the language with a greater awareness of culture and customs – and can provide **real** opportunities for speaking and listening. It's also a great source of free language-learning resources!

Language-learning situations can be found in your local high street, although visits abroad provide the greatest opportunities. Without being too heavy handed or 'teacher-like', a lot of enjoyable activities can be built into a holiday.

At home

Once you have some idea of what to look for, spotting potential resources becomes a piece of cake!

PACKAGING

Find words in other languages on signs or packaging, e.g. *baguette, tortilla, pasta, croissant, spaghetti.*

RESTAURANTS

Look for foreign restaurants and ask yourself the following questions:

- What does the name mean? e.g. *Café du Bonheur.*
- What's on the menu?
- Is there a bilingual menu?
- Can you see some words which look familiar? e.g. *les carottes, caffe.*
- Have a go at speaking to the staff in their own language – even if it is only to say *'buenos dias'* or *'adiós'*!

SHOPPING

Play shops in the foreign language – remember to use euros!

DANS MON SAC

Take it in turns to add to an alphabetical list of what is in the bag:

Il y a dans mon sac ... un abricot;
une baguette;
un croissant;
une datte.

If played while in the country, this list could be built up over a period of time, as things for the bag are spotted.

FOOD

Make a menu in the language for a meal at home (as shown right).

Use a simple recipe in the language to cook something. Recipes designed for young children can be found on a number of websites.

MENU

HAMBURGER
FRITES
OU
UNE PIZZA
SALADE

YAOURT
OU
FRUIT
JUS D'ORANGE

Abroad

If you are lucky enough to go on holiday to the country where the language is spoken, this is of course a wonderful opportunity to collect materials and work with your child on mini-projects.

Even before starting out on your journey, you can encourage your child to research the places that you are going to visit, check the long-range weather forecast for during your stay and work out the stages of the journey. If you have access to the Internet, this will be relatively easy. If you do not have access to the Internet, your child might contact one of the national tourist offices. They are often very helpful, especially if specific information is requested. Some useful contact details to get you started are listed at the end of the chapter in the 'Resources' section.

Once you are in the country, there are many opportunities for you to draw attention to some aspects of language and culture. Listed below are examples of the sort of activities you can encourage the language learner to try out, together with suggestions for resource materials to look out for.

EATING OUT

Encourage the children to order in cafes for themselves and, as they become more confident, for the whole family.

SHOPPING

Ask children to check purchases from the supermarket against the till receipt when unpacking shopping.

SCRAPBOOKS

Build up a food scrapbook – it could include:

- bills from cafes;
- menus;
- postcards of foods;
- interesting packaging and labels;
- supermarket leaflets.

More general scrapbooks can be fun to keep – they might include:

- public transport tickets;
- entrance tickets to museums and other places of interest (**1**);
- postcards;
- maps and town plans;
- tourist brochures (**2**);
- hotel brochures and bills (**3**).

Once a scrapbook is underway, it provides a good starting point for picking out some simple words or phrases that occur regularly and may become familiar. In French tourist leaflets, for example, the following key words constantly reoccur:

Entrée	entry ticket
Tarifs	prices
Horaires	times
Ouvert	open

As you visit places of interest on holiday, it can be fun to look out for some of these key words and to find others, and perhaps have a competition to see who can spot the most! This will help to reinforce new vocabulary.

MENUS

Menus can be fun to keep and look at. Ice cream menus from hypermarket restaurants, for example, are particularly good as they have clear illustrations. In some restaurants the menu takes the form of a place mat which gets thrown away. Once you have a menu or two, you can talk about the dishes, compare prices and even do some simple role plays in which you take the parts of waiter and customer. When you are looking at a menu with your child, count out the prices with some real money. This helps them to get used to handling unfamiliar coins and notes, and also provides an opportunity to practise the numbers in the foreign language.

PHOTOGRAPHS

Setting up a little photo project is popular with some children. This could be as part of, or instead of, the scrap book idea. A disposable camera, for instance, gives children the freedom to take pictures that interest them. This can be a real record of the actual places that you are visiting and could even be arranged around a specific theme, such as:

- shop fronts;
- street names;
- advertising posters;
- signs and notices.

BOOKS

There are enough visual clues in comics to help convey the meaning. Read through together to see if you can recognise words and phrases or use the pictures and context to help you work out what they mean.

Browse in a bookshop. Look at the picture books – books written for younger children may have a structure and language level which is just right for early language learners (see 'Using books and other published material', p39).

Drop in to the library for a look at their selection of picture books.

MAGAZINES

Buy 'activity' magazines which contain art and craft activities for younger children. Often the language is simple and following the instructions to make something provides a really purposeful activity in the language – and it's great fun!

TOURIST OFFICE

Visit the Tourist Office in the town. This can be an excellent source of free material such as bilingual leaflets, maps and plans, posters and postcards.

DIRECTIONS/TRAVEL

Encourage your child to develop his or her map-reading skills – and practise their words for directions by getting them to guide you round the town.

Visit the station or bus station. This can again be a great source of free material – leaflets, timetables, etc – and a good opportunity to pick up some simple vocabulary for times, leaving and arriving, platforms and place names.

what parents say ...

Holidaying in France gives a real reason to learn the language and with a bit of extra input of the sort suggested here, the children certainly seemed to pick up extra language, which hasn't been the case in previous years. It was great fun to make a scrapbook up and we like to look back on it – using as many French words as we can, of course! My children were a bit shy of ordering in cafés, but once they got over that and realised that they could be understood, they loved it; they also got into the habit of going to buy the baguettes and croissants each morning. This year's holiday really is the first time that they have shown any real interest in the language, and I think that is down to us making a bit more of an effort with speaking French.

(Parent of Jamie, 9, and Nathalie, 11)

tourist offices in the UK

French
French Tourist Office
179 Piccadilly
London W1J 9AL
Tel: 020 7493 6594

German
German National Tourist Office
PO Box 2695
London W1A 5TN
Tel: 020 7317 0901

Spanish
Spanish Tourist Office
22/23 Manchester Square
London W1V 3PK
Tel: 020 7486 8077

Italian
Italian State Tourist Office
1 Princes Street
London W1B 2AY
Tel: 020 7408 1254

resources

eleven

Through the year

A good ongoing project which makes links between language and culture is to find out about how the year's festivals are celebrated in the country whose language you are working on. Some of these will clearly be the same festivals as ours, but there will be others which it will be fun to find out about – and give an excuse for an extra celebration!

The following section suggests some activities for Christmas and there then follows a calendar of 'special days' celebrated in France.

Christmas

SEND A CARD

Look out for Christmas cards bought in this country which have greetings written in a number of languages. In many European countries, however, it is more common to send cards at New Year rather than at Christmas (see right). It can be fun to design and make your own cards using one (or more) different languages.

BONNE ANNÉE
ET
MEILLEURS VOEUX

Here are some phrases you may like to use:

	French	German	Spanish
Happy Christmas	Joyeux Noël	Frohe Weihnachten	Feliz Navidad
Best wishes from	Meilleurs vœux de	Herzliche Grüsse	Muchos recuerdos de
Happy New Year	Bonne année	Frohes neues Jahr	Feliz Año Nuevo
Father Christmas	Père Noël	Der Weihnachtsmann	Papá Noel

Titre : Nouvel an planétaire
Carte fournie par Mona Daly

À : Anne and David

Chère Anne et Cher David,

Je vous souhaite à mon tour une très bonne année 2001 en espérant que cette nouvelle année vous apporte la santé, le bonheur et la concrétisation de tous vos souhaits les plus chers.

Grosses bises à tous les deux !

Valérie

- valerie Dray

Send an Internet Christmas card. There are many sites that will enable you to do this (see 'Resources' section at the end of this chapter).

A CHRISTMAS SONG

Christmas songs can be found in many collections in books, on websites and on cassettes or CDs. It may be easiest to start with one whose tune is already familiar. This version of *'Douce nuit, sainte nuit'* can be found on the website **www.momes.net/comptines** where it is even accompanied by a recording of the music.

Douce nuit, sainte nuit

Douce nuit, sainte nuit
Dans les cieux, l'astre luit,
Le mystère annoncé s'accomplit,
Cet enfant sur la paille endormi,
C'est l'amour infini, c'est l'amour infini.
- Paix à tous, gloire au Ciel
Gloire au sein maternel.
Qui pour nous en ce jour de Noël,
Enfanta le sauveur éternel,
Qu'attendait Israël,
Qu'attendait Israël.
- Saint enfant, doux agneau.
Qu'il est grand, qu'il est beau.
Entendez résonner les pipeaux,
Des bergers conduisant leurs troupeaux
Vers son humble berceau, vers son humble berceau.

CRAFT ACTIVITIES

Mix a festive craft activity with some language learning. Books, magazines and websites designed for young children will make a point of using very simple language for instructions and often use a combination of word and picture lists of what materials are needed for the activity.

CHILDREN'S WRITING

Children's writing can be found in many places on the web and is often very accessible because of its simple language. The poem on the left is one such example and can be found on the site **www.jecris.com.**

Noël est proche
Noël approche

Noël c'est la fête
Noël est dans ma tête

Noël c'est pour toi
Noël c'est pour moi

Noël est sans chagrin
Mais Noël n'est pas sans sapin.

COOKING AND FOOD

It can also be easy to find simple recipes in books, magazines and on websites. Look out for recipes for food that is typically eaten in the country at Christmas, such as *Stollen* in Germany or *panettone* in Italy, or look for the finished product in the supermarkets! You can try Aldi, Lidl and Waitrose which sell everyday German foodstuffs and of course *Lebkuchen* and *Stollen* near Christmas.

Try a *bûche de Noël* (a Yule log) or at New Year the *galette des rois* with the fun of finding the *fève,* or token, which earns you the right to become king or queen for a day.

A calendar of French festivals

January	February	February	March/April
6 — Fête des Rois	St Valentin — 14	Mardi Gras	Dimanche de Pâques

April	May	May/June	May/June
1 — Le premier avril	Fête du travail — 1	Fête des Mères	Fête des Pères

June	July	December	December
21 — Fête de la Musique	Le quatorze juillet — 14	Noël — 25	Fête de la St Sylvestre — 31

6 January Twelfth Night or Epiphany	**14 February** St Valentine's Day	**February** Shrove Tuesday	**March/April** Easter Sunday
1 April April Fool's Day	**1 May** May Day	**May/June** Mothers' Day	**May/June** Fathers' Day
21 June Festival of Music	**14 July** Bastille Day	**25 December** Christmas	**31 December** New Year's Eve

Bringing it home

what parents say ...

We picked up a free calendar in a supermarket in Spain. We've had fun looking at it, and we've learnt the months and the days in Spanish together. We've also noticed that they have more national holidays than we do, which the children think is unfair. It has helped to keep their interest in Spain and Spanish going though!

(Parent of Ailsa, 10, and David, 8)

books | French

Mon grand imagier des fêtes. Flammarion (ISBN 2-08-160590-2).

Collin, M. *Une année en imagier.* Père Castor Flammarion (ISBN 2-08-160898-7).

Two books which contain information, activities and games for celebrating the special days in the French calendar.

websites | French

Many websites can be found simply by entering key words such as *Noël enfants* into a French search engine such as **yahoo.fr.** Some websites containing simple writing, pictures, songs and activities connected with Christmas

that are particularly well designed and interesting are:

www.vive-noel.com

www.perenoel.com

www.universdelulue. free.fr

www.momes.net.

www.jecris.com/TXT/NOEL

www.coindespetits.com/ fetes
This site contains more general information on websites.

websites | German

www.weihnachtsstadt.de
This site has songs, recipes and ideas for making decorations and an advent calendar.

www.german-way.com/ german/christmas.html
This site has recipes, Christmas e-cards and carols.

www.bingo-ev.de/cgi- bin/ub/tannbaum
You can use simple German language to personalise your own Christmas tree.

websites | Italian

www.californiamall.com/ holidaytraditions/ traditions-italy.htm
Gives information on Christmas in Italy and recipes.

resources

www.navidaddigital.com

www.christmas-world. freeservers.com/ spain.html
This website contains information about Christmas in Spain.

www.fiestasatope.com
This site has a calendar of Spanish festivals.

Other websites enable you to send greetings cards on-line, such as:

http://fr.greetings.yahoo. com

www.weihnachtspost karten.de

www.postales.com

www.santas.net/howmerry christmasissaid.htm
This website shows you how to say 'Merry Christmas' in over 80 languages.

resources

twelve

Key points

As we pointed out in the introduction, the enjoyment of the language-learning process is central to most schools' aims and it is vital that this aspect is treated equally importantly in any activities at home. Whereas the learning of lists of vocabulary and the chanting of verbs may have been what parents experienced as homework, it is certainly not appropriate at this level.

To summarise, the key points to bear in mind as you aim to build up your child's ability and confidence in the foreign language are:

■ Always introduce the spoken form of a word or expression first. Let children see the written form once they are familiar with how it is spoken.

■ Build the language into your daily routines wherever possible.

■ Find opportunities to use the language for real communication.

■ Buy or find materials that are appropriate for the language level of the child. This may mean that the content is aimed at a younger child.

■ Use your computer (or the one in the library!).

■ Use songs and poems – try to include some tapes and videos by native speakers.

■ Wherever possible make links with other languages spoken at home.

■ Find out what your children are learning at school – but don't feel that you must follow slavishly. Anything you do which encourages enthusiasm about learning the language will be beneficial and welcomed by the school.

■ Make use of all the foreign language opportunities around you. These include packaging, menus, media, foreign football players and words to songs.

■ Make it fun – for you and your children!

Appendices

thirteen

Alphabet pronunciation guides

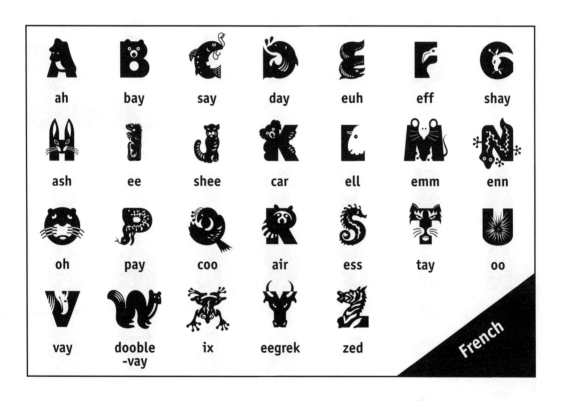

ah	bay	say	day	euh	eff	shay
ash	ee	shee	car	ell	emm	enn
oh	pay	coo	air	ess	tay	oo
vay	dooble -vay	ix	eegrek	zed		French

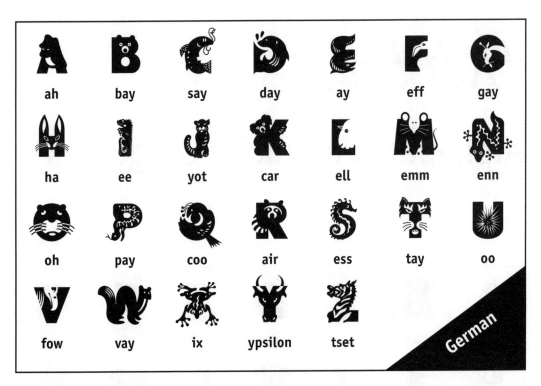

ah	bay	say	day	ay	eff	gay
ha	ee	yot	car	ell	emm	enn
oh	pay	coo	air	ess	tay	oo
fow	vay	ix	ypsilon	tset		

German

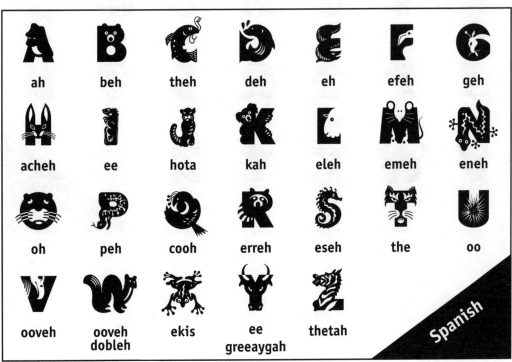

ah	beh	theh	deh	eh	efeh	geh
acheh	ee	hota	kah	eleh	emeh	eneh
oh	peh	cooh	erreh	eseh	the	oo
ooveh	ooveh dobleh	ekis	ee greeaygah	thetah		

Spanish

fourteen

Further sources of information

- The National Advisory Centre for Early Language Learning (NACELL) is housed by the Centre for Language Teaching and Research (CILT) and has an excellent website, full of information and recommended resources, of use to parents and teachers: **www.nacell.org.uk.**

- The National Curriculum for England, Modern Foreign Languages is downloadable from the Qualifications, Curriculum and Assessment Council's website: **www.qca.org.uk.**

- The non-statutory guidance for Modern Foreign Languages in Key Stage 2 (7–11 years) is also available from QCA.

- The findings of the Nuffield Inquiry into the national capability in Modern Foreign Languages in the UK are available via: **www.nuffield.org.uk.**

- Information on the Welsh Assembly Government National Foreign Languages Strategy is available via: **www.wales.gov.uk.**

- Information about languages teaching in Scotland can be accessed through Scottish CILT: **www.scilt.stir.ac.uk.**

- The national languages strategy for England *Languages for all: languages for life* can be downloaded from: **www.dfes.org.uk.**